Hiding Gay

Hiding Gay

We all can overcome our adversities only when
we accept the hand the GOOD LORD has
dealt to us

John Vaglica

Library of Congress Control Number:		2010909140
ISBN:	Hardcover	978-1-4535-2568-5
	Softcover	978-1-4535-2567-8
	Ebook	978-1-4535-2569-2

This book was printed in the United States of America.

To order additional copies of this book, contact:
Xlibris Corporation
1-888-795-4274
www.Xlibris.com
Orders@Xlibris.com
82422

This book is not intended for all audiences. Although it is free of vulgarity, it is explicit in some areas, and it is intended for mature readers.

Dedication

This book is dedicated to all mothers of gay children but especially to my mother – a wonderful, caring, and nurturing person. I have always felt that mothers of gay children do not have to be told of their children's sexual orientation, but in fact, they somehow *just know*. I will tell you how I know my mother knew I am gay. I never told her, and she never embarrassed me with what I suspect she knew.

One year while my mother wintered in Florida, I thought I would bring my partner Kirk for my usual weeks' vacation and he would have an opportunity to meet my mother and my sister, Rose. Kirk and I had a great vacation, and the time with my mother and Rose was wonderful. Whenever my mother and I spoke after that vacation, she would always ask how Kirk was. At one point in Kirk's and my relationship, we separated and went into couples counseling. The next time my mother asked about Kirk, I informed her that we were not together. Her response to me was "Well, dear, maybe you'll find another young man to share your life with."

Mother, this book is dedicated to you. I love you with all my heart. Thank you for not embarrassing me with your maternal instincts and knowledge.

Acknowledgments

SOME OF THE wonderful and incredible blessings of my life have been the outpouring of support from the few people I can really call true friends that I have met in the path of life and also my siblings. These are the people who have helped me overcome the mountain of adversities I have fought and won. Some just listened, and some gave advice. Since I came to terms with my sexuality, with the help of these few friends and siblings, I never felt as though I walked alone. For those few friends and siblings, I will remain forever grateful. This book would not be possible because as you will read, I thought the end should come. I discovered through faith that God saved me for three delightful reasons in addition to the wonderful partner he introduced to me seven years ago.

I also must give accolades to my editor, Janetta Messmer, with all her patience and understanding. I also owe many thanks to my critique partner, Merry Foxworth. May God bless you, Merry, for all your English lessons on proper punctuations. I want to thank all the new acquaintances I have met in this journey of book writing at my Monday-night writers/literary group named Write Ingredients. My thanks to you all.

The people who have helped me on this difficult but incredible journey are too numerous to mention. I would not be where I am today, alive and well, without the love and support of my mother, my siblings, and as I mentioned previously, the few friends I have met along this wonderful road.

And finally, I am thankful and grateful for the many blessings God has bestowed upon me. I know there have been times I was not deserving of his goodness and the bounty I have received, but I believe he has unfailing love.

Prologue

WHEN I ORIGINALLY began writing this book, it was for revenge. I began writing to tell all the people in Houston, Texas, all about the injustice in our judicial system. I wanted everyone to know what happened to me because of a vengeful and morally corrupt judge that used his power and his bigotry. Then I realized I would be as vengeful as he is, and I do not want to become that person.

Furthermore, my story is not about losing a trial, and it is not about a vengeful judge. Also, it is not about a corporation that claims to be nondiscriminatory. It is not about a corporation that refused and failed to provide me with a safe work environment. It is about bigotry and prejudice. It is about people growing up in an era when you could not be the person you are in your own skin.

Being gay in the '50s and '60s was almost a death sentence. This book is about that exact pain and stigma assigned to homosexuals of that era. When you have finished reading this book, I hope it will give you an insight as to the adversities I have overcome. I hope you will know from the fight that I fought that these adversities have brought me to the GAY person I am today.

I began writing this book prior to the events of the West Virginia mining tragedy of April 2010. The weekend of April 11, 2010, following the tragedy, President Obama was on the news expressing his condolences to the families of the tragedy. My story can in no way compare to the loss of twenty-nine lives. However, President Obama made the statement that everyone in the United States deserves a safe place in which to work. I was denied this human right, and I was the one that paid the price by having to give up my career that I had worked so hard to attain.

I knew our society had failed me and I knew our judicial system had failed me miserably and I knew I had a story to tell. What I did not know was that it would take two years for me to get medically well enough to finally sit down and tell my story about a corrupt and prejudiced judge using his bench against a protected class of human beings. What I did know was that one day I would get well with my medical and psychological issues because I am a survivor. I knew that one day I would be willing to take on the bias and prejudices of a federal judge without fear because I would no longer be HIDING GAY.

Chapter 1

FROM VERY YOUNG, I'd dress up in girls' clothes; and with my older sister, Rosemarie, we would sing along with Perry Como, Rosemary Clooney, Patti Page, and other singing stars of that era who sang on the radio. We would pretend to be a sister act. What fun we had. I also remember when my other brothers and sisters called me a little girl. I didn't care; it was fun playing dress-up with my sister Rose. We were a team. This went on for a while until just before I grew into double digits. I knew the dressing up had to stop. The name-calling and shame associated with it began to be more than I could handle. Then my father's rejection – the final straw. I knew I was different from my brothers, but I didn't know why. My older brother Phil liked to hang out with the guys; I did not. My younger brother, Bob, was a great ball player on a little-league team that my father coached. I had no interest in any sports. Yes, I knew I was different.

I can remember when I was twelve years old. My father had my seventeen-year-old cousin come to live with us. He had problems at home, and I think Dad thought he might save my cousin. As if we didn't have enough kids of our own. I was one of seven at the time. My brother Tom came along later, in my eighteenth year. Anyway, I shared a room with three other brothers, so my cousin made a fifth person in an already overcrowded bedroom.

One summer evening, I decided to go to bed a little early. Shortly after, as I was lying in bed, my cousin showed up and said he wanted to go to bed early also. I enjoyed watching him as he undressed and got into bed but immediately dismissed the thought. My cousin and I had some brief conversation and then silence. All of a sudden, my cousin said, "Hey, John, give me your hand." Not thinking anything of it, I obliged. I found my hand wrapped around his penis, and he was showing me how to ejaculate him in the darkness of the bedroom.

This was my first homosexual experience, and the memory still lingers – the warmth and wondering how soon it would be over but not wanting it to be overcame me. I really enjoyed what had just happened.

As I lay there, the enormity of the situation hit me. What had just happened? Did my cousin make me do this? If someone finds out, I'll tell everyone he made me do it. What would I tell my two best friends? We were always together like the Three Musketeers. David was the better looking of the three of us. He was tall and slender of build with straight black hair. When he left his home every day, he sparkled with cleanliness and neatly ironed clothes. His family was of Jewish religion, as was most of Newton. I recollect fantasizing about having sex with him someday, although I did not how he would accept such an offer. I did not think he was gay. Ben was stout of build with unkempt hair. His daily attire consisted of a jersey and khaki pants. I never thought of having sex with Ben, although I never had the idea that he may be gay. Both families owned their own business and were quite comfortable.

In my day, you were disowned by your family, friends, and anyone else IF THEY KNEW THE TRUTH. You were sneered at and labeled FAGGOT OR QUEER. I had to keep this secret.

As time went on, I tried not to be alone with my cousin. I knew I would enjoy what I might allow to happen. My cousin would be going into the navy soon, and I would not have to worry about that happening ever again. One night that fall, I stayed at my aunt's house for the weekend. I learned that my cousin was at my grandmother's house about a mile away that same weekend. I called to ask if he wanted to come over, which he did. He knew what I wanted, and I knew what he would like as it had developed into something more than manual stimulation by this time.

It happened over and over. I knew I had to hide this dark world I would be living in. At that age, I could never have imagined or realized what adversities were truly ahead of me. I could never have imagined what coping strategies and skills I would need to develop or the many years of counseling it would take to get me where I am today.

Chapter 2

MY PARENTS WERE both extremely hardworking folks. My mother held a full-time job working the three-to-eleven shift five days a week. She was a group leader in the cable department working for a government subcontractor that I went to work for many years into the future. My mother did this in addition to raising eight children. As you can imagine, her days were quite busy with laundry as well as tidying up the house. Before going to work each day, my mother would also start dinner for the family. My sister Rose was expected to finish cooking the meal after returning from school.

My father worked two jobs for as long as I can remember. After leaving his full-time job as a government subcontractor, he would then go to work part-time, usually at convenience stores. There was a brief period when my father started his own produce business. His first store in Brookline, Massachusetts, proved so successful he decided to open a second store in Wayland, Massachusetts. The expansion did not prove successful as one store's profits began draining on the other store. The business closed about seven years after it opened. Also, my parents' responsibilities never allowed time for themselves to take vacations alone. Usually, vacations consisted of two weeks on Cape Cod with the entire family.

Due to my behavior during my adolescence, I never felt as though I measured up to my father's expectations as his other sons did. Many of my years between the ages of ten to fourteen, I spent summer vacations with my two old-maid aunts, my mother's sisters. While there, I was expected to take care of my aging great-grandmother and help with all the housework. At first, I objected to being shipped off to spend summers in this type of environment. Then I began to realize that I was living the life of an only child. This meant that I was showered with clothes my parents could not afford to provide for me as well as many other luxuries. I was being indulged for the services I provided.

One day, I overheard my elder aunt on the phone. She was telling another aunt how wonderfully I cleaned her house. She went on to say that she was certain I would not object to going to her house one day a week to clean her home. At thirteen or fourteen years old, I remember being infuriated with this expectation or assumption. I also remember having a crush on this aunt's youngest son, Tommy, who was at least five to six years older than I was. I didn't want him to see me cleaning his mother's house. Yet I obeyed my aunt's request and went to clean the other aunt's house, being very cautious should Tommy ever go home from work early. I always hoped that I had left for the day before he went home.

One day, he came home from work early. I was totally mortified that he saw me in this situation. Those feelings of being considered "a little fairy" crept in. I'm cleaning his mother's home instead of playing ball like other young boys my age are. Tommy was in no way gay, but quite the contrary very masculine. He worked with his father and other brothers in their family business. He never mentioned seeing me clean his mother's house. I really enjoyed the times when he would pay attention to me.

I called my parents to explain my feelings about being used as a maid service for other relatives. I asked to go home for the remainder of the summer. Both my parents agreed to my request, and my father picked me up the next day. After that, I never was expected to go to my two aunts' homes for summer vacations. The one thing I knew I would miss was not seeing my cousin Tommy, although he never knew the feelings I had for him.

Chapter 3

BY THE TIME my cousin entered the navy, I was in junior high school or, as it is known today, middle school. I knew I had to keep my secret. I also knew that my cousin was not going to let anything be known about what happened; after all, he was going to be a macho sailor. To this day, I have never put any blame on my cousin. First of all, I feel if my initial experience had not been with my cousin, it would have been someone else as I was most likely ready to enter into the homosexual lifestyle. Second of all, homosexuality is not a choice; one is born homosexual.

I was in seventh grade at Weeks Junior High when I found out that a girl named Marylou was interested in me. There was a junior-varsity dance coming up, so I thought if I asked her out, no one would suspect my dark secret. Marylou and I went to the dance and had a great time. I also enjoyed watching the football players dancing with their dates for the evening. No one ever suspected or at least asked, so I felt secure. Over the next year, things seemed to go pretty smoothly. The Three Musketeers kept hanging around together. David and I talked about dating and the girl thing. Ben was not interested in girls but in no way appeared to be QUEER either.

By eighth grade, David started dating Sue, and I hooked up with her best girlfriend Judy, both from well-to-do families in Newton, Massachusetts, where I was raised. Sure, we did the crazy things guys do when they are fourteen years old with their girlfriends. Friday nights were always make-out nights in Judy's living room with David and Sue, Judy and me. Halfway through the night, David and I would compare notes to see who scored the most. Judy's parents even paid for me to take professional dance lessons with her. Since our family was so large, my parents could not afford the lessons. We also did the school dances and many other social activities, but in my heart, something was always missing. I wanted a relationship with a man. Then the fear and shame would wash over me, and I would bury the desire again.

In ninth grade, the Three Musketeers split to two. Ben's family moved from Newton to Belmont, so it was just David and me. We continued to date Sue and Judy for a while and then as always, there was the split-up. The girls went their way, and David and I went ours but remained strong friends. After all, we had been friends through Mason-Rice Elementary School, Weeks Junior High, and would be looking forward to going to Newton High School together. Or would we? Newton built a new South High School, and the dividing line had not yet been determined. The bad news came halfway through ninth grade. I missed South High by one street. David would be going to Newton South, and I would be going to Newton North. As high school began the first semester, I could feel that the friendship David and

I once had was slowly diminishing. By mid-freshman year, our socializing faded to a minimum. By year's end, it was only a memory. It was not planned; it just happened.

I never heard from David after high school. And for many years I wondered what had became of him. One day while running some errands with my daughter, when she was about three years old, I happened to be in my old neighborhood. I decided to stop by David's house to see if he still lived there. He did, and I introduced him to my daughter. David had never married. We chatted for a while, and then I said I had to be on my way. That was the last time I ever saw him. I have looked for David at great length on the Internet, but to no avail. I have always felt that I would like to know what became of him and the future he built for himself. I often wonder if he ever suspected that I had feelings for him, other than that of being buddies. Currently I have been looking for him on Facebook although unsuccessfully.

Chapter 4

HIGH SCHOOL INTIMIDATED me. I had this fear down in the pit of my stomach that my sexuality would be challenged. Now more than ever, I felt I must put up this façade. My plan: I migrated toward the upper classmen and the jocks in hopes that I would appear more macho. And my desire for the male gender became stronger with each passing day. My head told me I needed to spend time with girls to keep my secret hidden.

In the halls, my eyes kept glancing toward the male body parts. It seemed it was something that was beyond my control. As I continued to look, did anyone suspect my secret? What was I going to do if they did? How could I stop this insatiable desire? Thoughts of suicide became an overwhelming option.

I didn't date much in high school; I only dated enough to keep those questions from being asked. When relationships got too close, I would break them off. I hung around with my older sister Rose and her friends quite a bit and began to date a friend of hers named Debra.

Debra had many future plans for us even though I was only seventeen. Her plans included how many kids we would have. She decided how long we would date after I was out of high school before we would get married. This scared the living hell out of me. Needless to say, after several months, I broke it off with Debra. This dating scene was working really well for me now and I had managed to keep my secret. No one would be calling me a QUEER or a FAGGOT.

After I broke off the relationship with Debra, I took some time off from dating. In a couple of months, I began dating another one of my sister's girlfriends. By this time, I was in my senior year of high school. Although I did not know at the time, this friend of my sister's would be the woman I would fall in love with and marry.

Dating Lynn was fun, and we had a lot of things in common. I kind of put the cousin issue and the "GAY" thing on the back burner and just concentrated on us. Although I must admit, my eyes did wander toward the male gender's private parts quite often; however, I never did respond. But it wasn't easy.

Lynn and I belonged to a Christian youth organization with a local church group. The joining of this group was prompted by Lynn's mom because she felt that it would be important for our spiritual well-being. She was a dedicated, devout, and practicing Catholic. The organization held many activities including ski weekends to the mountains in Vermont and New Hampshire. These activities were great fun, and I remember enjoying staying in the all male chalets. I knew now that I had to be extremely cautious as this was not only a Christian youth organization but that it also included many of our friends.

Lynn and I married in 1964, when I was twenty and she was twenty-two. Our first child, a girl, was born in 1966. Life seemed good. I dismissed most of my "homosexual" thoughts and the rest of the times busied myself with projects around the house. We had, by most standards, a good marriage; and I was able to keep my secret.

My wife was a stay-at-home mom as we owned a two-family home in suburban Boston, which afforded her that luxury. We were very close with my wife's parents, spending a lot of free time with them. I even held a position in the same company where my father-in-law was an assistant plant manager.

Many of our vacations were spent traveling with my wife's parents, and I thought of them not only as a second set of parents but also that they were great people. Friday nights were the nights we would go food shopping after dinner. We enjoyed her parents' company so much that after we put the groceries away, we would stop by her parents' house for a couple of drinks and conversation. They adored our daughter, their only granddaughter. Lynn's sister only had three sons.

Our second child, a son, was born in 1969. We named him after my wife's father. Life at home was just okay, however, and sex at home was seldom at best. Thoughts of sex with other men were on the increase and becoming uncontrollable. One evening, my wife and I had a terrible argument. By this time, I had met some gay men through my position at work, although I'd never hooked up with any of them. When they would take me out for lunch, the conversation would always seem to end up with what may be going on in their lives. Several of the men invited me to go some evening with them to the downtown Boston clubs. I felt I needed to refuse.

There was one man in particular named Bill that kept inviting me to his apartment although he knew I was married. He often said if I need a place to stay, just give him a call.

After the argument with my wife, I left the house and made up an excuse, in my own mind, as to why it would be okay to call Bill – if only for someone to talk to. I knew what I wanted and I knew what would happen. I called Bill, who was elated to hear from me and anxious for me to get to his apartment.

I spent the night with Bill. When I got home the next day, all seemed to have been forgotten and forgiven regarding the argument. At least nothing was brought up. Not talking about the argument and my secret overwhelmed me. And with the shame I felt, I attempted suicide although I was not sure I wanted to die. The next day while in the Newton-Wellesley Hospital, I remember thinking that I was happy my wife had gone home and found me. The hospital would not release me without a psychological evaluation.

Again the shame of this homosexual experience was overbearing, and I retreated into myself. I buried myself into my job, my yard work that I enjoyed so much, and my family. I told myself the night with Bill never happened. By this time, I had worked my way up in the company to the position of office manager. Bill was an executive for one of the big trailer companies I did business with. I was positive Bill enjoyed bringing in the business profits from the company I worked for, so he would keep our secret.

Chapter 5

LYNN AND I enjoyed a fairly comfortable lifestyle. She was still a stay-at-home mom. Since she had her own car, she and her mom met a couple of times a week for lunch. We spent summer vacations on Cape Cod while still spending other vacations with her parents and both of our children. At this time, the company had offered me a transfer to Connecticut as an office manager for a larger plant. I discussed the transfer with my wife, and we decided to accept the job. I did not know how it would work out for my wife as she was extremely close to her parents. I thought it would be a good move for me. I could bury myself in my new job, and the thoughts of homosexuality would go away. I could not have been more wrong.

One of the men I worked with told me about this movie theater in old downtown Thompsonville, Connecticut, that showed XXX-rated movie flicks in the afternoon. I began to frequent this theater. I would find myself in the men's bathroom, where the unimaginable would go on. This began happening more than I cared to admit. I knew it had to stop.

My wife was unsettled about the move from day one. To appease her loneliness, we would go to Boston almost every weekend to be with her family and our friends. Less than a year after moving to Connecticut, I interviewed for and accepted a position with a government subcontractor back in the greater Boston area. I still kept my secret; no one knew I was HIDING GAY.

Lynn and I knew that moving back to Boston would mean she would have to give up being a stay-at-home mom. The price of homes in Boston was so much greater than that of Enfield, Connecticut. The salary that I was offered for my new job could not make up the difference in the mortgage for the home we selected. My wife got a job at the local bank four days a week. The kids were enrolled in private Catholic schools, and life seemed good again.

I knew this would be better – a new job, a new company and a new start. I would dismiss all thoughts of homosexual relations, or so I thought. I started at my new job in December of 1973, where I met Ronald, who worked in the cost accounting department. Ronald immediately picked up on the fact that I was GAY. He was not interested in a relationship but wanted to be friends and said he would introduce me to a couple of places where I could go to meet other gay men for a rendezvous. Ronald took me to a place called the "bird sanctuary" in Cambridge, Massachusetts, on the banks of the Charles River. The second place was the tower by Norumbega Park in Weston, Massachusetts.

THIS WAS THE WORST THING THAT COULD EVER HAVE HAPPENED TO ME.

From that day forward, I was on a downhill spiral into the seedy life of a homosexual lifestyle. It was a place where you met men in the woods and behind trees for sex. These rendezvous left one feeling dirty with guilt.

I was putting my new job on the line, and I could not control my appetite for male sex. I would go to the "bird sanctuary" or the tower in the morning then return sometimes at lunch and perhaps after work. On Sunday morning after church, I would grab a cup of coffee and go sit by the Charles River, hoping for a hook-up. Most of the time I was successful as everyone else was there for the same reason. I met my dentist there from time to time, former neighbors, several coworkers, and even a relative. We knew no one would ever say anything.

These two cruising areas were strictly for homosexual activities. Every once in a while, the police would show up, and we would scatter as if we were roaches in the night when a light is turned on. Sometimes there were the unlucky ones that got caught.

I always seemed to have an angel on my shoulder. Someone was always watching out for me. For all the years of promiscuity, for all the morning times and lunchtimes and times after work and Sunday mornings after church, I never got caught by the police. Worse yet, the unthinkable, I never got AIDS, HIV, or any other social disease.

Thoughts of the diseases ran through my mind, but I could not stop my appetite, my passion for sex with other men. What would I tell my wife if I did get HIV or AIDS? I did not have a clue. I only knew the drive for sex with men was so intense that I would cross that bridge when and if I had to.

Chapter 6

BRINGING UP MY son and daughter was a joy and a challenge as any parent will tell you. Both children, after they finished third grade in public school, entered private Catholic schools. My wife and I made this decision because if a student was not in a private school before sixth grade, they were not guaranteed a seat by then. The middle school and high schools in our city were tough schools for exceptional students to attend as these students were abused by the less fortunate.

My daughter excelled in everything, both academics and sports, and was an honors student all the years at St. Patrick's. Every year, from the beginning of fourth grade, she continued to receive medals and awards for her excellent achievements. My wife and I attended spelling bees, where she would win second place, if not first. Every year, her science project was selected along with nine others for a presentation at the school in the evening, for other parents to observe. During the early to mid-eighties, one local

Boston television station had a program titled *The Best of the Class*. With my daughter's high academic achievements, she was shown on television as the best of the class for her school.

Although my son was exceptionally bright academically and good at all the sports he played, he enjoyed being the class clown. At times he would deliberately act out in class to get his classmates laughing or just to see if he could push the teachers' buttons. Then my wife or I, or both of us together, would be called down to the school regarding my son's behavior.

I re-collect one meeting that we were called to the school regarding my son's behavior. In attendance were three of his teachers and the school principle on one side of the table. On the other side was just my wife and I. Every one of the school representatives kept telling us how badly my son behaved in school. Upon leaving my wife made the comment to me that she felt as though we were against a firing squad.

My son also had many good academic accomplishments. He too had his many nights of recognition for outstanding science projects and mathematic competitions.

It was determined that my son acted like this because he could not compete with my daughter's reputation for being an exceptional student. Every year his teachers would say, "Oh, we hope you are as bright as your sister." My wife and I knew he was, but we needed another mechanism to allow him to shine.

As any parent can tell you, if your child goes to a private Catholic school, you are expected to be involved in all the fundraisers, which we were. This also helped to defray some of the operating costs of the school, thus keeping tuition costs lower. I was also president of the school organization for two consecutive years, so that gave my son the idea that he had special privileges.

It was at this point that we decided to move my son to a larger all-male parochial school in Boston. The brother that interviewed us must have read my son's records and knew how bright he was. During the interview, he told my son, "If you think you are coming here to fool around, we don't want you." My son immediately buckled down to his schoolwork and became very comfortable at Catholic Memorial. There were four other boys from Waltham that went to this school, one of them being my son's best friend who lived next door. They had been friends since they were four years old.

My son did so well at CM and always went home from school and went right to his room to do homework. Second semester, he was on honor roll and took accelerated courses. He was doing so well we thought Catholic Memorial had sent someone else's son home to us. It was a complete one-hundred-eighty-degree turn for him.

He continued to excel at CM, remaining on high honors. Both he and the boy next door joined the hockey team as managers. Many of their friends played on the hockey team, as did one of their good friends, Jason. This was to be his future brother-in-law. It was through Jason that he met his future wife in their junior year of high school. During one of the hockey games, my son looked up into the stands. His eye caught sight of a beautiful blonde cheering on the team. He skated across the ice to where Jason was. My son said to Jason, "Who is that gorgeous blonde up in that seat?" Jason said, "Where? I don't see any good-looking blonde." My son pointed to the blonde. Jason said, "Oh, her, that is my sister." Eight years later, my son and his girlfriend became husband and wife.

Both my son and daughter continued to do well in school. My daughter was at St. Patrick's High School and my son was at Catholic Memorial High and all was good. It was my daughter's senior year in high school, and with her excellent grades and SAT scores, she was accepted to the College of the Holy Cross in Worcester, Massachusetts. In the fall of 1984, my daughter entered Holy Cross, and my son remained at CM for his senior year.

My son never wanted to transition from public school to private Catholic school after the third grade. Once enrolled at St. Patrick's School, he made every weekend a living hell. I think he felt so confined and restricted during the school week; he totally reacted negatively on the weekends. He didn't want to do any family activities and wouldn't go to church. Halfway through fourth grade, he decided to try out to be an altar server. He was accepted, and he passed all the training classes. Once he discovered how much I wanted him to follow through with this commitment, he dropped out of the program.

Every weekend was total chaos. Now I began to see my son's dark side. I felt somehow I had let him down in life. I was able to do all the things parents do to make a good life and indulge their children. What had I done to make this child so unhappy, so unappreciative?

My son could become extremely forceful, mean, and cruel when he did not get his own way. During the holiday season of his freshman year in high school, he asked if he could have a few friends over for a New Year's party in the family room. I told him that his mother and I were having some friends in for a party in the living room and he could have his friends in the family room. The understanding was there would be no drinking, to which he agreed. Halfway through the night, he came to the living room and said that one of the girls had gotten sick. We found out that there was quite a lot of drinking at the party. I confronted my son and told him to tell all his friends to call their parents to pick them up and go home.

My son got right in my face and said I had embarrassed him and then began pushing me with his chest. For the first time ever I was afraid of my son as he had become someone I did not know. I did not know if he too had been drinking and this was the alcohol talking, so I decided to just go out and take a walk. I waited until all the kids left and went home to help my wife clean the family room. Yes, I felt as though I totally lost all control of my child.

The next day, my son seemed to be quite remorseful of the previous evening. It was New Year's Day and, as is said, "What you do New Year's Day, you do all year." Lynn and I wanted to make this a good day. We suggested going out to dinner and making it a family and relaxing day. Everyone was in agreement.

All seemed to be going well for quite some time. My son was doing well at CM. He got his driver's license around the same time as all the other boys in our town that went to CM did. The boy next door had his own car, which was new, so my wife and I felt obligated to get our son his own car. A friend of mine at work bought himself a new car and asked if I wanted his old car for my son. I was most grateful for this offer.

Although the car was old, my wife and I had the car mechanically and aesthetically upgraded. My son was insulted to have to drive such an old dinosaur, as he put it, to school. He wanted my fairly new Cutlass Supreme. I gave in and let him have access to my Cutlass Supreme, and I drove the older car to work. Three months after I gave my son my Cutlass Supreme, he tipped it over on its roof in the Albemarle Brook due to speeding. I could only thank God he was not hurt, although the car was totaled.

What a mistake when you give your kids too much. I remember talking to my doctor about this very situation, and his great advice to me was "John, you and Lynn give away the whole farm when you should only give away what you are comfortable with." I did not take my doctor's advice even though I knew I should have. I trusted him because he knew my secret. I thought it was the intelligent thing telling my doctor about my sexuality.

So both my son and daughter continued to lead extremely privileged lifestyles. We vacationed on Cape Cod for many summers while the kids were growing up. The cottage was on a private island called Mashnee Village. Entrance to the island was via a causeway and was monitored by the police. The island had a private clubhouse with a pool for the residents that did not care to use the beach area. The clubhouse overlooked the pool, which allowed us to visit with some friends and family. We could enjoy drinks with them and watch our kids, all within eye distance and the safety of the lifeguard.

We also suggested the kids get interested in skiing because we thought it would help their social skills later in college and their professional lives. I prompted my son to get interested in golf at the age of fifteen. I also felt this would give him the upper hand in his professional life. He went on to qualify for many amateur opens.

Both our children went to private schools, wore designer clothes, and always had access to high-end vehicles to drive. They had to pay for nothing except the gas they used. My wife and I paid for everything else. They were not allowed to have their own vehicle until after college graduation because they excelled so well in school. We did not want them to have to work for a vehicle and allow their grades to suffer. Hence, we always had a family vehicle at their disposal. They did work a few hours a week for some spending money.

The only financial requirement we had for my daughter during her four years at Holy Cross and my son's four years at Bentley College was their minimal student loan and their book bill.

Even with everything handed to our children, my son became extremely aggressive with me between his junior and senior years in high school. It was on a Saturday morning, and we had another extremely volatile argument. The fight continued to escalate, and I decided to retreat to my bedroom. All of a sudden, my son came into my room in a rage, wanting to continue the argument. I tried to push past him, but he was too big for me to get away from. He is an athletic build of 5'10", and my slight of build and being only 5'6" didn't match.

He grabbed me from behind and put his arms around my chest. By the time I got away from him, I was hyperventilating. I grabbed the car keys and started driving up the street when all of a sudden I could feel myself getting dizzy and light-headed. I pulled the car over and got out for fear of having an accident. I was told by witnesses and the EMTs that I was holding on to my chest when I fell to the ground. I was taken by ambulance to Newton-Wellesley Hospital, where I spent three days.

A few days after the incident and my stay at the hospital, I received a very nice card with a letter enclosed from my son's girlfriend. To this day, I have saved her letter. I don't know why or if I just had a premonition. She apologized for his behavior and extended her love for both my wife and myself. She proceeded to say that "with love, we all can work through this." From then on, I knew my son had a violent streak that was uncontrollable.

My daughter did not do well during her first semester at Holy Cross. The first report that we received during Christmas break showed she was on academic probation. This infuriated me, but I knew if she had gotten herself this far, I wanted her to graduate from a prestigious college such as the College of the Holy Cross.

She worked during Christmas break. When she got home, I made it clear that if her grades were not brought up to my satisfaction by summer, that when she was saying good-bye to her friends at school that spring, it would be for good.

I also let her know that I could be paying state-college rates and not private-college rates for what I was getting. She clearly understood, and the party girl was left at home when she went back to Holy Cross.

My son did remarkably well from day one at Bentley College, as both his mother and I knew he would. He lived in his first year but was not really happy with dorm life. He spent more time at home than at the dorm as we only live one mile from Bentley. There were many nights that he came home for dinner, and he would bring at least one or two friends to join us.

There also were times my wife was doing his laundry and she would find some clothes half his size. He took pity on one of his roommates when he ran out of money and couldn't afford to do his own laundry.

The last three years of college, he lived at home and continued to do extremely well, remaining on the dean's list all four years. My son graduated in 1991 with honors and decided to go right on for his MBA. This was a decision both his mother and I supported.

His only concern was whether or not it would be right to expect his girlfriend to wait another three years before marriage. My son and future daughter-in-law got engaged and set a wedding date for June 1994. Everything was okay, and I still managed to keep my secret.

Chapter 7

MY SON AND future daughter-in-law were engaged for three years before their big day in mid-June 1994. During that period, my son finished getting his MBA in finance and accounting. He continued living at home until he got married in order to save the money for their new home, which was completed a few months before the wedding. However, Lynn and I convinced him to move in before the wedding rather than leave the new home empty for several months. For a house warming gift, Lynn and I gave the kids a new $1100 refrigerator.

The wedding was extraordinary and lasted well into the morning hours. Both my son and daughter-in-law needed to be congratulated and were congratulated by both families for the excellent job they did in planning and hosting the wedding. They spared nothing and paid for the entire wedding themselves. Again, Lynn and I wanted to give the kids something nice for them to remember as a wedding gift. We told them to go to the furniture store of their choice and pick out a complete living room set, which they did.

Relatives came from everywhere, some staying at our house. Life was good. After the wedding, my son and his new wife settled into their new life.

Then two months after the wedding, the unthinkable happened. I got caught by the police in one of the cruising areas. Oh my god, what would I tell my wife? By the time I got home, she knew as the police officer had already called her. She was waiting there with my son. As you can imagine, the scene was chaotic at best. My son called his sister to come over as there was a family issue that had to be discussed. I had to come clean and confess. My daughter arrived, and we talked about what had happened. She was not as upset as I thought she might be and seemed more understanding as to what happens with life today. My son's last words to me that night were "You are disgusting and a disgrace to this family. Get yourself to a doctor and get this fixed now."

Let me tell anyone reading this book; **YOU DO NOT GET "GAY" FIXED**. You are either gay or straight.

Believe me from my heart; I have tried. If I told myself once during this lifetime, I have told myself over again that I don't want to be this way. I have thought to myself over and over again that I will stop all this cruising. It only lasts for a very short time. But the desire is so great, it is so overwhelming that a gay person will always find the relief they need, that place to go.

If they tell you they have stopped or that they are not going to those dark places, they are lying to you. What's even worse, they are lying to themselves. I DIDN'T WAKE UP ONE MORNING AND SAY "OH GEE, I THINK I WILL HURT THE PEOPLE I LOVE THE MOST." Gay people are born this way. It's not anything our mothers did, so don't play the blame game there. I hold no animosity toward my cousin either. More than likely it was just time to wake up my homosexuality. It is the way we are wired, and we have to live our lives the best way we can. Get over it; accept us or move on.

The morning after I got caught in the cruising area and my son told me to get myself fixed, the filth, shame and guilt rushed over me. I didn't know what I wanted to do. I knew I didn't want to put in another night like the previous one. Again I thought suicide was the only answer. If I got rid of myself, then everyone would be better off. The next morning, I left for work as usual and waited down the road for everyone else to leave the house. I returned and parked in the garage but left the motor running. I waited in the garage for over three hours. At one point even getting out and lying under the car. I wanted to die to the core of my being. I never wanted to have to face my family again. I never wanted to have to see the looks of hatred on their faces again.

While I lay under the vehicle and the time passed, I could not understand why I was not nodding off into calming sleep. I realized after forty-five minutes to an hour that this was just not working. Our garage in the house we had built just the previous year was two and a half cars wide. It also had exceptionally high ceilings due to the three levels of the home. I began remembering this and thought I somehow needed to reduce the space my physical body was in. I got up and got a canvas to put over the trunk of the car. I then lay back down and just waited.

This attempt at suicide was just not happening. Next, I remember hearing my son speaking with the neighbor across the street from me. He had returned home as his house alarm was going off. I looked out the window of the garage. I thought, *Oh please, God, don't let him come to my house and find me here.* He left, and I remained in the garage for another hour or so.

I realized God must have another plan for me. I just didn't know what it was at the time, but he always has a plan if I lived through this ordeal.

My daughter accepted my sexuality with more of an open mind. She seemed to understand that this was a part of life although not completely happy with the fact that it was becoming a part of her life. She always treated me with dignity and respect although at the time I knew I did not deserve it. Thankfully, nothing changed between her and me. Before the incident, we would go out for a coffee and a muffin; we continued to do the same. Every now and then we would meet before going to the health club just for some private chat time. I have always loved and appreciated her for this acceptance, and she still made me feel like her dad. Because of my daughters acceptance of my sexuality, my son has not spoken to his sister for twelve years. She has made many attempts to have a relationship with him, but he will not respond to any of her pleas.

But with my son, from the time I got caught in the cruising area right up to the present, he has told everyone that he is where he is today because of only one parent. I know he knows the truth, and if making a statement like this makes him feel good, then so be it. I can only feel sorry for him because I know the truth also.

Shortly after the turmoil of getting caught, my daughter met the man she thought she was going to spend the rest of her life with. He was a naval officer from Arizona. My daughter had a professional career with a firm in Boston. Life was good for her at the age of twenty-nine, and the love of her life was thirty-two. He was in specialized training in California and went home for the holidays of 1994. He had to return to his base in Japan immediately after.

My daughter found out shortly after the holidays that she would be expecting their first child. Two months into the pregnancy, she was informed by the navy that he had been killed during night maneuvers in the Sea of Japan. Their child, a son, was born in September 1995. He was the light of the world to his mother, my wife, and me.

I knew the day my grandson was born that God had saved me from my suicide attempt to share in the fantastic life I would enjoy with this beautiful grandson in it.

The first three years of my grandson's life was as though I had been reborn. My daughter traveled extensively during this period. Her career brought her not only throughout the United States but also to Europe and Asia. During my daughter's travels, which sometimes consumed half a month or more, my grandson lived with my wife and me. What pure pleasure having him in our life. I no longer wanted to do any of the gardening that I so looked forward to doing on the weekends. My free time now evolved around this beautiful child and his daily wishes. That usually involved a morning and afternoon trip, pushing his stroller to the two local parks, where he scampered and played. We named one of the parks Bemis and the other Fitzgerald. I would ask him each time we left the house which one he wanted to go to. He knew the way to each, and if I tried to fool with him he would say, "No, Grumpy, the other way." If an airplane flew over the park while he and I were there playing, he looked up and would say, "There goes Mommy's airplane."

With the numerous emotions that have evolved because of my sexuality, I have never changed my feelings of love for my children and grandchildren. I show no favoritism in my weekly prayers at church for each one. My prayers at church include that everyone in their families find the love and respect for each other to be the family that the GOOD LORD and I want them to be. In addition, I ask that they enjoy a life of health, happiness, and prosperity.

Chapter 8

MY WIFE AND I had many discussions regarding the situation of my homosexuality, and she said at the time that we would work through it. We would seek counseling and work on our marriage. I began seeing a counselor, but I knew it would be very difficult for her as she was a very private person. In the end, my wife never sought counseling, but I was in counseling for over four years while the situation at home got worse.

I got caught one more time in a cruising area where I should not have been although not in a compromising situation. I was at the tower in Weston near Norumbega Park. While sitting on the ground, looking out at the Charles River, a man walked up to me and asked if he could sit with me. We were having a short conversation, and all of a sudden, he moved closer. My instincts told me this was not a good situation. I immediately stood up and said, "I am not comfortable and am going to leave." I took a few steps forward with my back toward the man. He stood up after a few seconds and introduced himself as a police officer. He informed me this was a sting operation and he was placing me under arrest. I said, "What for, I didn't do anything." He said, "Oh, yes, you made an advancement toward me." My daughter came to the police department in the town of Weston to bail me out.

The next day, my son said he called the town of Weston and spoke with the chief of police. He said the chief told him that I had my hands all over the officer and that I asked him if he wanted to have sex. Later that day, I drove to the Weston Police Department to speak with the chief myself. The chief informed me that he never had that conversation with my son because that is not what was written in the arrest report, and that was not what the officer said happened. Naturally, my wife had to believe our son because what he says has to be gospel. It was at this time that he also told me what a sick individual I was and that he was going to call all my family and let them know about me. I told him I would not give him the chance.

I immediately went home and called all my brothers and sisters to inform them about my homosexuality and the adversities I had been struggling with. I also told them about my son's threat. They all embraced me and were sorry I was having these issues but said they loved me because I am who I am.

The homosexuality issue was more than my wife could handle. There began a series of innuendos in the evenings that went on for months. My wife and I separated in March of 1998 and subsequently divorced in April of 2000. I have never blamed her for wanting the divorce. Not many wives want to be married to a gay man. She is a strong woman, and I am sure the embarrassment overwhelmed her. I know she had many thoughts of how she would discuss the reasons why we were getting divorced, not only to her family, but our friends.

Two of our supposed friends lived directly next door and were husband and wife. They are also parents to my son's best friend. The husband was a great guy and never could do enough to help a neighbor. The wife, on the other hand, had to be the first to know all about what was happening in Waltham. Her family was, at one time, very high profile.

She consistently would assure you of her friendship by inviting you out to dinner or for drinks. Before you knew anything, she had picked up the tab. The social gatherings and parties had to be held at her house. Somehow she managed to befriend you to the point of you allowing her to discover what was going on in your life. If the happenings in your life were hurtful to you, or even at times shameful, she had to be the first one to "tell all" to the rest of "Waltham" and, of course, all your friends. Somehow she was informed of my sexuality and the situation between my wife and me. Within days of her discovery, the entire city of Waltham knew about the "fag" living next door to her, and poor Lynn, as she put it. It was at this point that I told my wife to be careful with what she said to her so-called friend next door. I said, "She is not your friend."

People like my next-door neighbor have always amazed me. Her brother, whom we associated with from time to time, felt the need to expose his bigotry and prejudice to my younger brother. After learning of my sexuality, he visited my younger brother, who worked at Home Depot in Waltham.

Her brother was not a friend of my brother's, nor did they even socialize. He made it a point to locate my brother at work for a conversation.

Then he proceeded to say to my brother, "Gee, it's too bad John is like THAT." I would like to know what "THAT" means. I do not understand why there is no compassion from people like this, and they seem to find a need to kick you when you're down. This world would certainly be a better place without the bigotry and hatred that are placed upon those who may be different. Perhaps people of a different sexual orientation, race, or religious belief would not have had to hide in the shadows most of our lives.

I always felt like one of my wife's children instead of her husband and lover. She treated me wonderfully with material things; in fact, she treated me better than wonderfully, but that was not what I needed. I needed someone that was more aggressive in the bedroom, and that was not her passion. But then I was always told it was the manner in which I presented myself. I also knew that what my wife needed was a husband that was totally honest about his sexuality, and in my days, that is what gay men feared the most.

I must, and I do, take total responsibility for the breakup and breakdown of our marriage because I wasn't forthright by not being honest. I have often discussed with my counselors the facts of me screwing up my wife's life.

Perhaps we should never have met and married. That is something I am not sure of. I believe God makes everything happen for a purpose. The one thing I am sure of, gay or not, is that without me, neither of us would have the two bright and beautiful children we have or the three grandsons we have been blessed with. I loved her then, and if anyone can believe it, I love her today. She is a wonderful mother and an even better grandmother.

A few months after my wife and I separated, I received a second letter from my daughter-in-law. This letter I also saved and have to this day. She wrote to state her feelings and emotions regarding my wife's and my separation and my sexuality.

She expressed how much she loved us both but that she loves her husband with all her heart and soul. I totally respect this passion and devotion. She then proceeded to tell me that I had no right to marry my wife and have children.

I do not know why she felt it necessary to get involved and write a letter like this. I told her that both she and my son should remain neutral and not get involved. I further stated they should treat me in the same manner as I have treated them, with dignity and respect. Perhaps I should write back to her and ask where she would be today if it were not for me. I am quite sure she would not be living the lavish lifestyle she enjoys. She would not live in the grand, beautiful house she enjoys, nor would she be the wife of a CFO and vice president of a corporation. She would not drive the Lexus SUV she enjoys or have the Corvette for a toy. I know she would definitely not have the diamonds, emeralds, and other jewels that are abundant in her life. Most of all, she would not have that fantastic son she is raising and raising him very well, I will have to say. My daughter-in-law has stated to me many times that she has a very cushy lifestyle and is not going to do anything to upset it.

Would this mountain I am climbing ever become just a hill?

Chapter 9

SHORTLY AFTER I got caught in the cruising area by the police, I changed jobs from the government subcontractor to a major computer corporation located in west suburban Boston. As far as my professional career was concerned, I felt I had reached utopia. I landed a job with a computer giant at twice the salary I was making previously. I was now working out of the area where no one knew me. I worked for a company that valued my opinion and wanted my input, unlike what I was accustomed to at the government subcontractor.

My professional life was on top and my home life was in the toilet. My daughter's career excelled, and the company she worked for had asked her to relocate to Houston, Texas. She accepted the offer, and in February of 1998, she and my three-year-old grandson moved to the fourth largest city in the country. When my grandson left Boston, I felt as though my life ended. He was my only link to happiness at that point in my life.

In June 1998, the computer giant that I worked for was bought out by another bigger computer giant located in Houston, Texas. Life still seemed good, and my career was very exciting and successful. I noticed no cultural change in the transition between the two computer giants. I continued getting more project assignments, and with the recent takeover by the Houston-based business, I wanted to prove myself worthy.

In November 1999, my manager came to me and asked if I would consider a transfer to Houston, Texas. The corporate headquarters was looking for program coordinators, and he recommended me for one of the positions. I had never informed anyone at work of my home situation because I always kept my private life private. I briefly explained that my wife and I were separated. If she chose to pursue the divorce, I would welcome the opportunity for a change.

I notified my manager that the divorce was final in April 2000, and by June, I was house-hunting for my first home as a single GAY divorcee in the Houston suburbs. By this time, my daughter had relocated again, to the Dallas suburbs.

My son and his wife were expecting their first child in October 2000. My son had told me before I left for Houston that although I had not gotten my homosexuality fixed, he would not keep my grandchild out of my life. For that, I was grateful.

Life would be good in Houston, Texas. No one in Houston knew my secret, and I would not let anyone find out. Best of all, I was out from under the strain and finger-pointing of my now ex-wife but especially my bigoted, unforgiving, mean, and evil son. The continual finger-pointing of "This is your entire fault" every time I saw them. I could totally understand the feelings of my ex-wife. Her world had been turned upside down. She learned she was married to a total stranger, a GAY man. Someone she did not know.

I am sure she wondered where her life was going. I can also understand my son's immediate feelings at the time. He had just learned of his father's homosexuality, which I am sure was, to say the least, a shock to him. Also, my ex-wife told me that he feared "gay" would happen to him. As I stated before, you are either gay or straight; one does not become gay. Here we are sixteen years later, and the hatred and bigotry are worse than ever, which will take another chapter to cover.

I picked out a great brand-new twenty-two-hundred-square-foot home for myself; got moved in; and reported to work on July 8, 2000. I finally made it all by myself. A great job with a private office and employees reporting to me and a brand-new home. No one knew my secret.

Life was not good; it was great. I remember how good it felt to wake up in the mornings and get ready to go to work. I remember the excitement I felt to work for a company that valued its employees' ideas and opinions. Every day was a new experience, and I could not wait to start the next day.

I recollect how wonderful it felt to drink my cup of coffee in front of my garage, looking out at the park across the street in the morning with the sun on my face.

I enjoyed being a valued member of the server-storage team in Houston. Then I would get in the truck, back down the driveway, and go to work where I was wanted.

The joy I experienced coming home to the beautiful house I bought for myself and the fun I would have decorating it was overpowering. Then I wondered if I would ever have anyone in my life to share all this with. I immediately dismissed that thought as life right then was all too busy. But I did want someone to share all this with as I was lonesome. I told myself that would come sometime later. Right now I had to concentrate on work and the house. What was most important to me was that no one knew my secret.

Right away, I was assigned my first project with a peer named Tim. The project was so enormous it was divided into two sections. Tim had the larger "EL" portion of the project and I was assigned the "CL" portion. Tim and I got along from day one. Tim had more experience coordinating a project build than I had. Server projects began with the first printed circuit board through to the design of the mechanical box and everything in between. The projects I managed in Boston involved sending an engineering design to an outside vendor. Yes, Tim was my crutch on this first project, and I thank God that I had him for a peer and on my side. I am sure if I hadn't, I would have turned tail and ran back to Boston. Anyway, I stuck it out. Thank you, Tim; you are the best.

Tim and I successfully launched our first project together. The server-storage business unit held a launch party at a local club. It was a great fanfare to a great team. I felt wonderful for this success. Tim and I got separate projects from then on but worked within the same business unit. All our assignments were going well and proving to be a success. During and at the end of each assignment, I was getting awards for outstanding performance. Life was good, and no one knew my secret.

By the time I relocated to Houston, my daughter and grandson were living within a four-hour drive north of me. Visits were about every other month. By now my daughter had met the second best man to enter her life (the first one being my grandson's biological father).

Visiting my daughter and her family was always fun and interesting. Of course, seeing a grandchild is always a grandparent's delight. My daughter and her husband always made the weekend fun by taking us to interesting places in the North Dallas suburbs.

The end of the weekend always saddened me and my grandson as separation seemed overbearing. I would drive down the driveway and watch as the little boy waved good-bye to his grandfather, and I knew that he was sad and sometimes crying.

Little did everyone know, I cried halfway home and then some of the night after I reached my home. Three years into my daughter and son-in-law's marriage, they had a son together, whom I love very dearly. My daughter, her husband, and two sons still reside in a North Dallas suburb. I visit them several times yearly, and the boys spend two weeks during their summer vacation with me as well as part of their Christmas and spring breaks.

I start making plans for the boys' vacations with me long before I am going to pick them up. I want to be sure I have in the house all the special foods they enjoy eating. Kirk and I plan the meals that we will be eating at home. Cooking is Kirk's specialty. Mine is cleaning. Perhaps if I didn't have Kirk cooking for me, I wouldn't be so fat; oh well. Anyway, then I start planning activities. My oldest grandson is a creature of habit. His favorites are Schlitterbahn Galveston, arcades and bumper cars, and of course, the movies.

The youngest one needs to wake up and put on cartoons in his room. At the end of the day, he thoroughly enjoys a bath in my garden tub and, of course, needs all his tub toys. As long as those needs are fulfilled, he is happy with anything else we do. When we don't have activities to do away from the house, they both enjoy the pool. Every New Year's Eve, we have to go to Olive Garden for dinner, without fail.

Chapter 10

SOON AFTER MOVING to Houston, I was inquisitive enough to want to discover what everyone was making insinuations and innuendos about this place called the Montrose. One Saturday, shortly after my move to Houston, I got dressed up and ventured out to the Montrose. I thought I fell into a candy store for gay men. Here I was right in the center of this medley of bars, men, and loud music; oh boy. I had a beer at each bar, and by the end of the evening, I was a bit tipsy. This was my first experience with the gay lifestyle in Houston. I remember how wonderful I thought all the gay clubs appeared and that I had met some really nice people.

In an effort to keep my secret, I thought it necessary to make an attempt to do some dating with women. For the first few years I dated three women and enjoyed going out with each one. I also knew this was just a cover up for what I did not want people to discover.

Immediately after moving to Houston, I met the constable of my subdivision under unfortunate circumstances. I had gone out to the clubs on a Saturday evening and had quite a bit to drink. I was on my way home at about 2:30 a.m. My thought was at this time of the morning, no one would be around. After entering my subdivision, I blew through the first two stop signs. The next viewing in my rearview mirror was the rolling lights. I was pulled over and asked for identification. I explained to the officer that I thought no one would be here, and he said, "But I was." He said he detected a very heavy scent of alcohol coming from the truck and would I step out.

I obliged, and upon exiting my vehicle, I fell to the ground. Needless to say, I was given and I failed a sobriety test. The officer then introduced himself to me as Brian. He then said, "Here is what I am going to do. I am going to give you a ticket for failure to stop only because you are already in your subdivision. I will escort you home to put your vehicle in the garage, and then I will give you your license back." When we got to my house, I thanked him as I realized I was extremely fortunate. The next day, I saw his cruiser across the street in front of the park. I walked over and asked him if I looked any better than the night before. He said, "John, you look a whole hell of a lot better." I reiterated my many thanks to him again. My daughter suggested that I also buy each one of his children a gift for Christmas, which I did.

In January 2001, I met the new constable in our subdivision. I thought that the cruiser I was approaching might have Brian in it. After realizing it was not, I said, "You're not Brian." He introduced himself as Mike, the new full-time constable, and I told him my name was John. I was on my way home from work, so our conversation was brief, but I noticed that he was drinking a Dr Pepper. I invited him to stop by anytime he was in a slow period for conversation and a Dr Pepper as I always had that particular soft drink in the house. He told me he was in the midst of a very messy divorce. I also gathered from the conversation that he was quite comfortable in his sexuality as a straight man. He made that point clear although I did not know if he picked up at this time that I was gay.

I became very good friends with Mike, and within a short period of time, we were confiding our innermost thoughts for advice with each other although I was still HIDING GAY. By the end of the second week, Mike asked if I was interested in experiencing some of the Houston cowboy nightlife. That sounded exciting, and it would be a thrill to be experiencing it with none other than a cop, how cool. We went out every Friday and Saturday nights. I will say that unbeknown to Mike, there were times that I still found time to meander downtown to the streets of Montrose.

Mike showed me a side of Houston that was like going to Las Vegas. The clubs, the loud music, and the dancing (and with women, no less), this was the life. Oh yes, I could go to work on Monday mornings and have quite a story to tell all my coworkers. No one would ever guess my secret now. I was running around to all the cowboy clubs in Houston every weekend with a macho cop.

About four to six months into the friendship, I was very comfortable with my new friend, but I was also beginning to feel very guilty. I decided it was about time to tell him that I was gay and let the chips fall where they may. I knew he would be calling soon, and I knew what I was going to do. The phone rang, and it was Mike. We got into a short conversation, and I finally said, "I need to tell you something." He said, "If it has anything to do with 'DON'T ASK, DON'T TELL,' I will make it easy for you. I have suspected for quite some time that you may be gay, and I don't care.

"I like you for you and I enjoy your company. Your sexuality is your business, okay. Does that make it any easier?" I thanked him for that.

Mike and I no longer do the club scene on the weekends. As a matter of fact, he is no longer a constable. He is now the owner of a successful swimming-pool business in the Houston area. He is also married, and he and his wife enjoy the son they had together in July 2009. I was quite honored to be asked to be best man in his wedding, to which I accepted. The gift I received for being his best man was a watch with the inscription "Best man once, friends forever."

By spring of 2001, I met Richard at one of the clubs in Montrose. He was not quite twenty-one years old. I was extremely flattered by all his attention but also fooled that someone so young could be interested in having a relationship with a man my age. Richard and I dated for about four weeks. His previous lover, who was fifty-three, called him while we were at my house one Sunday. Richard went running out of my house like his ass was on fire. I decided at that moment – enough of dating the twenty – and thirty-year-olds. The world was too much about them, and I did not need that immaturity invading my space. I continued to go to the Montrose every once in a while meeting some very nice people. I also met some not-so-very-nice people.

Occasionally the local hustlers would find their way into the bars. Usually the bouncers knew who they were and would escort them out the door. I was not street-smart. I was grateful for this level of security.

About a year and a half after Richard and I split, I met Joe at another one of the bars in Montrose. Joe was in his forties, and we hit it off right from the start. He worked for the school department in Cypress, so his workweek was busy with school. We were together every weekend from Friday to Sunday afternoon. I thought life was fine and Joe would do almost anything I asked. He enjoyed dining out as much as I did, and we would try different restaurants every weekend. He also enjoys driving, which I do not. We would go for many long drives in the country and around Lake Conroe. He lived with his sister and did not like that arrangement.

He wanted more than I was willing to give as far as living arrangements for him. That relationship lasted about five months, and Joe decided he needed more from a mate. Joe asked if he could move in with me. This was something I was not ready for and we decided it was best for the two of us to take some time away from each other.

Several months later, I met Sean, who was in his fifties. At the time I met him, he was a pianist in the Houston Symphony. I thought this was the guy for me. Sean was about 6'4" tall with salt-and-pepper hair. Being with the Houston Symphony, he had a lot of culture and charm. We dated for a while, but he had aspirations of moving to Austin, and I was not about to relocate. We ended our relationship on a friendly note. I hear from him every once in a while, and he is happily living in the Austin area.

Quite a while after Sean left for Austin, I met Kirk, the man I am still with today. We met January 30, 2004, at a bar in Montrose that is known to be a biker-leather club. I had always been apprehensive about going into this club, but little did I know that reputation proved to be a fallacy. The patrons were as tame as pussycats and also very cordial. When I saw Kirk, I walked over and asked him if he would join me for a drink. He was extremely shy but suspecting, so he said, "Let me think about it." I told him he needed to make a decision soon as I was on my way out of the club, headed home until I saw him standing alone at the bar. I went back to where I had been sitting, and a few moments later, he walked over and asked if the invitation for the drink was still open. We had a couple of more drinks, exchanged phone numbers, and I left for home.

I called Kirk in the middle of the following week for a date for the next weekend. He accepted, and we met at the same club. We dated for a while and decided it was time to move in together in my home. To this day, I keep reminding Kirk about his statement, "Let me think about it," and we both have a good laugh.

Our first couple of years together got a little tumultuous at times. We separated for a while but then decided to give our relationship another chance to work things out.

After about a year and half later, we mutually agreed to separate for a while but sought couples counseling, which worked well for the both of us. I discovered that I was not as perfect as I thought I was. The counseling also brought out some skeletons from our past that made us what we are and how we deal with and accept situations that occur in our life.

Kirk and I are still together today working toward our seventh year. Thanks to the counseling we received, we are better equipped to understand each other. We know each other's weaknesses and strengths and feed off that. I sold the larger home that I owned when we met. I downsized into another new home, and we are very comfortable living in the Woodlands.

Chapter 11

ANYWAY, I HAD my weekend life and my professional life. I still managed to keep my secret, and that was how I wanted it although there were so many times I wish I could have told Tim. At one point in early 2001, I began feeling pretty comfortable with the group I was working with in Server Storage. I thought perhaps this would be the time to come out in my professional life. I could stop living a double life and finally be myself, in the skin I was comfortable in.

Soon after I was having these thoughts of "coming out," I was in a managers' meeting in our director's office. After the meeting, a couple of managers, including myself, stayed back for some small talk. Somehow, the conversation came around to a gay software engineer that worked on the eighth floor. My director said, "I have nothing against THEM, just don't push THEM off on me." I immediately dismissed any thoughts of coming out as I valued my career too much, and that surely would have been a career-leveling move.

Although the corporation claims to be "GAY FRIENDLY" and nondiscriminatory, that comment from my director scared the crap out of me.

I still have former work associates that are gay and living with the fear of coming out or someone in the company discovering they are gay. The fear is that it would be a career-leveling move for them also. Somehow the excuse for your layoff is due to a "workforce reduction." The workforce reduction always ends up with someone else doing the job you once held, and not the fact the word got out you are gay.

I got assigned another great project in early 2002 that launched in mid-2003. It was a great project to work on, and I had a terrific team to help me get it launched and make money for the corporation. Just before the project launched, I was called into my manager's office for my next assignment. The business unit wanted me to make plans for a new project that would be starting up within the next couple of months. Life was good, and no one knew my secret. I was still *Hiding Gay*.

In November 2003, my new project began. This was to become my final project with the corporation although I was unaware of this fact at the time. Program management and engineering teams were assigned, and I held the kickoff meeting.

During the second meeting, the mechanical engineer who was assigned to the project became very agitated and boisterous toward me. As the project coordinator and facilitator of the meeting, I was able to gain control, and we proceeded with the meeting. I was unaware at this time that he suspected I might be gay. This fact was confirmed to me many months later by one of his support people. He told his support person that he could not stand the mannerisms gay people display.

Project assignments were given out for the next meeting, and I requested inputs for the project schedule. Some of the functions requested additional time for their inputs, which was normal as they had some lag time from other projects to complete.

The next week, some of the inputs for the schedule were handed in, and I said I would have as much of a project schedule completed as I could for the following week. This immediately irritated the mechanical engineer, who said he was accustomed to getting a project schedule at the start-up of a program and that it would be correct the first time. He wanted to know what was wrong with me and ask asked if I couldn't get anything right the first time. The program manager, who was present at this meeting, did not speak up and offer any assistance or defense for me or the manner in which the server-storage department carried out its projects. I told the mechanical engineer that this was customary for our business unit because some functions needed additional time to assign their limited resources.

During the first four to six months of the project, the mechanical engineer continually berated and bashed me at every meeting I facilitated. There was not one week that passed that I was not his target of abuse, and to make matters worse, the program manager never offered any assistance in my defense.

When I would ask him to step in and put a stop to this abuse, he would always say "Oh, that is just his way." Well, I found out that was his way of behavior all his professional life.

The woman that sat across the hall from me worked with the mechanical engineer at another company and said he was a bully at that company also. When she and another friend of hers from that company found out that this particular mechanical engineer might be hired by our corporation, they informed Human Resources of his past.

Early in 2004, headaches and panic attacks started to control my life. I also began to dread the thoughts of the days when there was going to be a project team meeting. I never knew what type of attack the mechanical engineer was planning toward me during that meeting. There were meetings he would call me stupid or ask how many times I had to make out another project schedule. There were also times he would ask what was the matter with me and was this my first project and then laugh.

In May 2004, I had what my doctor called my first syncope episode, which is a blackout spell and the onset of migraine headaches. This occurred as I was leaving my dentist's office. By the time the EMTs arrived, my blood pressure was erratic and spiking, and my pulse was elevated. At the time, I did not connect my work stress and issues I was experiencing from the mechanical engineer with my medical problems. My doctor asked me what was going on at work. When I told him, he connected the two issues. Along with the headaches and panic attacks, I began having severe episodes of depression.

I went to upper management and told them of my medical condition. The program manager said he would speak with the mechanical engineer's manager. After several attempts trying to get the program manager to resolve the abuse directed toward me at the meetings, I discovered that he had never spoken to the mechanical engineer's manager.

I immediately brought this to the attention of my direct manager. He said he was unaware of the situation and would speak to the appropriate manager that day, which he did. That did not resolve the situation. A week later, I spoke to my manager again and said that his meeting with the manager didn't result in stopping anything.

At this point, nearly a year of this type of abuse had passed. My syncope episodes had increased dramatically, as did the migraine headaches and panic attacks. I was sinking into a deeper depression.

I was not only seeing my primary-care physician, but he sent me to a neurologist for the migraine headaches, a psychologist for therapy, and a psychiatrist for depression. By now the co-pay for ninety-day prescriptions was over $600. My work life severely suffered, and I felt as though I was losing hold of my life and my career.

I told my manager what I wanted was a meeting with the mechanical engineer, his manager, Human Resources, my manager, and myself. I wanted to clearly discuss the situation, and if the mechanical engineer could not stop this abuse toward me and the distraction at my project meetings, he should be fired or, at the very least, removed from the project. Human Resources informed me at that time that if I continued to become ill, or remained ill, that I was eligible to go out on a medical leave. This was one option I did not want to do. When I relocated to Houston, my health was perfect.

My manager suggested that I give him the opportunity to have one more meeting with the mechanical engineer's manager and inform him of my request, which I agreed to. The next morning, the mechanical engineer came to my office and asked if we could talk. I agreed, and he came in and sat down and apologized, which I accepted. I told him we had a project to finish and we needed to behave in a professional manner for the team and the project. He agreed and left my office.

Two weeks later, I was facilitating a meeting with some of the vendors on the project and some of our team members. The purpose of the meeting was to resolve a problem where the mechanical parts were being built. People were making suggestions for a resolution to the problem, and I offered my suggestion. The mechanical engineer stood up and said, "Are you being stupid again, John? Screw you, I am not going to do that." I stood up, picked up my belongings, and left the meeting. My former manager saw me on the way back to my office. He had heard what was going on, and I informed him of what had just happened. He suggested that if the corporation was not going to create a safe work environment for me, I needed to notify the EEOC and file a complaint through their office. He said that his wife had gotten satisfaction where she worked by filing a complaint through them.

The next day, I filed a complaint against the corporation and the mechanical engineer. At the time of the filing, my only request for a resolution was a written apology. The EEOC did their investigation and found sufficient evidence to grant me a letter of right to sue the corporation.

Chapter 12

I CONTINUED TO work the project, but with the depression and other medical issues I was experiencing, I knew the quality of my work was not to the standards of the work that I had produced in the past. It was not to the "standards in excellence and achievement" for which I had received seven awards for work over and above what was expected for the past projects I managed. My manager came by my office one day after the company heard from the EEOC. He said it was too bad that things had escalated to this point but that he could not talk about the EEOC filing. What he did say was that he apologized for himself as well as the corporation for not doing something about the situation sooner and they should not have waited until I had gotten to the medical condition I was currently experiencing.

On October 6, 2005, I flew to Boston for my grandson's fifth birthday. Ever since my grandson was born in October 2000, I had flown there for Easter and his birthdays. With every trip, my son's animosity and bigotry grew worse, and he did not hide it. He would make comments to his mother like "I don't want people like that in my life," making sure his comment was within hearing distance of me. If I entered a room that he was in, he would leave. When I was there, he never spent time with me or asked if I wanted to go with him to run errands for his wife. And the weekend of my grandson's fifth birthday was the worst time I had spent in Boston since relocating to Houston. When I arrived that night he said to me, "Who is taking care of your dog, that transient friend of yours?" I said, "If you mean Kirk, yes, and he is not a transient person. He has a full-time job and is a contributor to the world." I knew at this point that my son had an agenda this weekend, but I did not know how bad the cancer and hatred had been growing within him.

By this time, my son had achieved the position of vice president and chief financial officer of his company. In this position, I am quite confident he has many gay people in his organization.

With this attitude, I should have immediately left with my brother Bob and gone to stay at his house, which I had done in the past. It was at my daughter-in-law's suggestion that I stay at their house so that I would have more time with my grandson. My brother Bob's house took over an hour to drive each way. When she made the suggestion, I had asked her if it was all right with my son. She said she would talk with him but was confident that it would be fine.

The next day was a Friday, and my son went to work. I spent the day with his wife and my grandson running errands for the birthday party and having lunch as we had always done in the past. That afternoon, my grandson took his nap, and I mentioned to my daughter-in-law that I thought I might get a workout in. She suggested that she get me some of my son's workout clothes. Unfortunately, I still had them on when he arrived home from work. He looked at me and said, "Where the f – did you get those clothes?" I told him that his wife had given them to me so I could work out. He told me I had a hell of a nerve wearing his clothes and to get my body out of them. Then he went into the room where his wife was and verbally attacked her. I felt really bad for her and was totally embarrassed and humiliated for myself.

The handwriting was on the wall as to what he had meant. He meant for me to get my "GAY" body out of his clothes. He made me feel as though I were a leper. On his salary he could have burned those clothes and bought fifty more outfits and not felt the loss of money. I went to my room a total wreck and called the airline to change my ticket to go home the next morning. I called my brother to explain what had happened and asked if he could go get me first thing in the morning.

After I got ready the next morning, I went downstairs with my suitcase. My son had left, and I told his wife that I was leaving soon and that Bob was coming to get me. I told her that I would not stay where I was not wanted and that the last five years was more than anyone should be expected to bear.

She stated that my son overreacted but that I should stay for the party. I said, "It's better this way." When my brother got back to the party, after taking me to the airport, he was talking with my ex-wife. She said, "I don't know why our son has to act like that." I said to Bob, "You wait. This will all turn around and be my entire fault." I left Boston on October 8, 2005, and on January 8, 2006, three months to the day I heard that my ex-wife said I should have sucked it up for our grandson and left after the party ended. Well, maybe I should have, but I was so overwhelmed with my son's actions from the night before I could not get out of Boston fast enough.

My son might have kept his promise about not keeping my grandson out of my life. But with all these negative events that occurred during my trips to Boston, he could not have made it any more unpleasant or made me feel so unwelcome. I left and have not been to Boston since. In the past five years, I have never missed the bigotry and hatred my son has displayed toward me.

What I have missed, and always will, is not having his son, my grandson, in my life. I have made the decision that I am a better person than the manner in which he treats me, and the last visit – I finally had enough.

Chapter 13

WELL, ANYWAY, AFTER that fateful weekend, I was back at work on Monday morning. My project kept me extremely busy because we would be getting ready to launch it soon. My health was still failing, and the tension between me and the managers was unbearable at best. Just before the holidays of 2005, my former manager came to my office. He apologized for what had happened to me and what he knew might happen to me in the near future. I asked him what he meant, and he said he could not tell me. He did say "If your case ever comes to a court trial, I will be willing to testify for you."

The holidays of 2005 were just around the corner, and I thought if I could just hold off until then, I would have two weeks to recuperate and try to get well. The frequency of the depression, migraine headaches, and syncope episodes that I experienced was beyond control. I thought that by the time I returned to work after the holidays, I would be the old John. I thought we would be launching my product soon, and the abuse would only be a bad memory.

Immediately upon returning to work after the holiday break, everything was just the same as it was before. There was the tension with the managers; the mechanical engineer was up to his abuse, and my health kept deteriorating. I had another meeting with Human Resources. The purpose was to discuss what the mechanical engineer had done to me regarding my health and also the corporation's lack of ability or refusal to provide me with a safe work environment. I was told that if I could no longer perform my duties, the option of leaving work on a medical disability was still available. On February 3, 2006, I left the corporation for the last time on a medical leave.

Shortly after I left on medical leave, I began wondering why it was me that had given up his career. Why did I have to stop driving down my driveway in the morning to go to a career that I looked forward to and enjoyed every day?

Why was it me that had to suffer at the hands of this abuser? Where was the corporation when I needed them and where was the safe work environment they said they offered and should have provided for me?

I never wanted to leave work at such a young age. All my life I was a healthy person, and I looked forward to a lengthy career. One day, I recall being in Tim's office. We were discussing the age we thought one had to retire. Neither of us was sure. I called our Human Resources representative to ask her. She stated there was no age limit for retirement. I told Tim it was my intention to work until I was seventy years of age. That is, until a work bully decided differently.

I had lunch with Tim shortly after my medical leave began. I decided it was time to tell him about my sexuality and informed him of my decision to file suit against the corporation. He said my sexuality was not an issue for him and that he loved my friendship and me just because I am who I am.

Between my siblings, Mike, and now Tim, I was able to come to grips with my sexuality and start living in the skin that I am in. I am relieved for my decision to come out to my friends and no longer am I Hiding Gay.

I began looking for a law firm that would support the EEOC's investigative findings that I had a right to litigation and answers to my questions regarding the loss of my career. After interviewing three law firms, I engaged the services of a downtown law firm just off the Milam Street exit. This firm began working my case in June 2006. My lawyer was confident we had more than sufficient evidence to win at trial. We had several meeting to go over the facts of the case beginning in November 2003 and the onset of my illness.

The legalities of the case began taking place, and the corporation engaged the services of another downtown Houston law firm. There were motions, depositions that kept going back and forth for over a year. I called my former manager that said if my case ever came to trial, he would testify on my behalf. He was not available at his home in Houston, but I did reach him at his home on Bolivar Peninsula. I filled him in on what was happening with my lawsuit.

I also requested that he have lunch with me and my attorney to discuss what he knew regarding my situation at the corporation, as we would like to take him up on his offer to testify for me. He said he would be back in Houston the following week and he would call me to set up a lunch date. He did not call me back, but I finally reached him by phone a couple of weeks later. He said he had a change of heart and would rather not get involved with lawyers.

The trial was set to begin in federal court on April 7, 2008. My lawyer began preparing me for the trial and reviewed with me what to expect. We prepared our list of witnesses, which included my former manager and my direct manager. The summons server went out to my former managers' homes in Houston and on Bolivar Peninsula. He said that both the vehicles were in the driveway at Bolivar Peninsula, but no one would answer the door. He further stated that he could also see the drapes moving in the windows. So much for the manager that would support me if my case came to trial but now was hiding behind drapes. My direct manager did show up for trial but as a hostile witness. He did state at the trial that he and the corporation's law firm spent two days the previous week reviewing his testimony.

The weekend before the trial was to begin, my lawyer wanted me to go to his home, in Walker County, both Saturday and Sunday to prepare for the trial on Monday. While reviewing the case with my lawyer, he said he had to take a break to call the finance person that worked up the numbers for my case. I overheard him tell the finance person that the reason the judge's first marriage ended was that his ex-wife was gay, but he used the repulsive terminology that "she was a carpet muncher." I knew what he meant. When my lawyer returned to the room I told him that I overheard what he said. At the time, I could not understand why my lawyer did not insist that the judge excuse himself from this case. Furthermore, if the judge had any integrity, he should have excused himself from this and any other case having to do with homosexuality issues.

I went to lunch with my lawyer on Saturday, in a restaurant where one might expect to find all the local residents gossiping. The restaurant, albeit small, served great meals. While having lunch, my lawyer brought up the subject of his brother. He stated that his brother was gay and suffering with HIV. His next comment to me was, "I don't understand this gay thing. You gays, lesbians and pedophiles, you're all the same." Here we were two days before the trial, and all I could do was move forward. Move forward with a biased judge and a lawyer that was afraid to ask the judge to remove himself for fear of retaliation in future court cases.

My lawyer and I continued to go over some of the facts of the case, and I learned that the judge was suppressing all evidence from November 2003 to October 2005. This was the period when all my problems of abuse, harassment, intimidation, and character bashing began, at the hands of the mechanical engineer, the bully. This was the period when I became ill with syncope episodes, panic attacks, nausea, and migraine headaches accompanied with bouts of depression.

My lawyer said the judge was not allowing this testimony to be heard because I am not in a "protected class." I wondered what that meant – I believed gay people became a protected class of people several decades ago and were not supposed to be the target of hate crimes. The only reason to suppress all the evidence from November 2003 to October 2005 was because of the judge's prejudice against gay people due to his personal situation. My lawyer stated that with all this evidence being suppressed, it would be a tough case but perhaps we could win. By now all seemed futile, and I just wanted to call it quits and go home.

Chapter 14

MONDAY MORNING, APRIL 7, 2008, came and jury selection began. The trial began with the facts of the case starting in October 2005 and the argument I had with my son. I did not have a good feeling as to what the outcome of the trial was going to be. The last day of the trial, the judge totally lost his integrity, character, and professionalism. When the trial was over and before the jury left for deliberation, he looked over at the opposing lawyer and said, "With all this going on, I can't imagine that Mr. Vaglica has not passed out." To this, she replied, "I agree, Your Honor." She too lost her professionalism.

The jury left for deliberations and returned within two hours. When we were summoned to the courtroom after such a short period of time, my lawyer said that was not a good sign. I also was not feeling very good about the verdict. The jury's verdict was read and was in favor of my former employer. Based on what the jury was allowed to hear, they could only have returned with the verdict they did. In my heart, I knew that my case would have had a different outcome if all the facts beginning from November 2003 were allowed to be heard. Unfortunately for me, our judicial system failed me miserably. Unfortunately for me, I walked out of the courtroom still on eight prescriptions a day. Unfortunately, I need to have quarterly injections in the back of my head, into my occipital lobes, for migraine headaches.

I felt as though a great injustice had been done to me, and I could not let it go without further investigation. I also knew that at the time I was too sick to look into anything. Or give my case the proper justice that was deserved. I took some time to try to recuperate medically and absorb what had happened to me. I tried to determine how I would get any of the facts pertinent to the judge and his divorce. A friend of mine worked for a legal investigative firm and got me the judge's case-file number regarding his divorce as well as the name of his first wife. I called his ex-wife and left a message to please get back to me. She did not, so I called her a second time and left a message as to the reason for my call.

The judge's ex-wife did call me back after my second phone call to her home. She appeared to be very pleasant and easy to talk with. She neither confirmed nor denied any facts of her sexuality. She did say that she had learned it was the judge himself that started that conversation in the lawyers' circles downtown regarding her sexuality. She also told me that the judge refused to give her any child support to raise their children and it was she who raised them on her own. She did advise me that I not continue with my investigation of her ex-husband. She said he was too powerful and that she herself could never come out ahead on matters relating to their children or their divorce.

I was beginning to feel overwhelmed with what this judge has been allowed to get away with.

I sent a letter to the directors of the Houston Bar Association and my state representatives. I did hear from one state senator's office and the Houston Bar Association, both denying any investigation into a federal judge's rulings. I did have an e-mail sent to me by one member of the Houston Bar Association, who is an attorney and former judge and friend of the presiding judge for my case.

The context of his e-mail was as follows:

From:
Sent: Tuesday, July 29, 2008 9:52 AM
To: vaglicajo@comcast.net
Subject: Re: Federal judge __ needs to be investigated for suppressing evidence in . . .

Mr. Vaglica,

Thank you for expressing your concern about a federal judge and the difficulties you encountered during your trial.

I have been a trial lawyer for almost 40 years. I know your lawyer and know him to be an excellent trial lawyer. I have also known this federal judge since his first appointment to the Texas State Civil District Bench [133rd District Court]. I have appeared before him numerous times in both State and Federal Court.

He is scrupulously fair and impartial. Further, I know his ex-wife very well and the correlation you assign to their personal situation is unfounded. In summary, if you were unsuccessful it is more likely that the medical testimony was not compelling.

Attorney at Law

I thanked this attorney for his response. I told him that my medical testimony was nonexistent as the judge would not allow the jury to hear it. I also said that the judge had an agenda for not allowing all the facts of the case to be heard. I let him know that I had spoken to the judge's former wife and that she had informed me about him not paying any child support for their children. And I said that this was coming from a judge that would lock up any deadbeat dads that didn't pay child support. I also told him that I was not surprised regarding his defense of the judge. His response to me was the following:

From:
Sent: Tuesday, July 29, 2008 2:32 PM
To: vaglicajo@comcast.net
Subject: Re: Federal judge __ needs to be investigated for suppressing evidence in . . .

Mr. Vaglica,

I have no wish to become 'pen pals' with you, but it is obvious that you have some issues that perhaps your psychiatrist can address.

When this federal judge was divorced he was a District Court Judge earning around $127,000 a year. His ex-wife, as a premier ophthalmologist was earning probably in excess of $300,000. Federal Judge D____ _____ could have, but didn't ask for contractual alimony from her.

Your reference to ' . . . all *you* people . . .' is offensive, but I am now learning is not surprising. Perhaps your attitude in front of the jury is why you did not prevail.

Attorney at Law

When I did not receive any assistance from the local media and my state representatives, I felt overcome with depression and desperation. I was a great fan of an afternoon show hosted by a famous doctor and his wife. In my desperate attempt to seek some help, I wrote to the doctor four times expressing my concerns regarding this crooked judge. The content of my first letter was as follows:

September 8, 2008

Dear Dr.

I was in litigation against my former employer back in April of 2008. Since then I have been investigating the federal judge extensively for his refusal to allow the jury to hear most of the basis of my lawsuit.

Since then I have sent e-mails to the local news paper and three local news stations as well as two of my state representatives. Additionally, I e-mailed the Houston Bar Association, all to no avail. I realize that most, if not all do business here in Houston and rub elbows with many famous downtown celebrities and socialites, so they are in fear of investigating the judge for a mere human such as me. I do realize that you also are from the

Houston area and are hopeful that you are not in the same position as the above mentioned. I have totally lost all faith in our judicial system and the willingness for anyone to let the truth prevail.

THIS FEDERAL JUDGE HAD AN AGENDA FOR NOT ALLOWING THE FACTS OF MY CASE FROM NOVEMBER 2003 TO OCTOBER 2005 TO BE HEARD. THAT REASON IS HIS PREJUDICE OF THE GAY POPULATION AND THE FAILURE OF HIS FIRST MARRIAGE.

You are my last resort and I hope that after reading my case you will help. I am attaching the string of e-mails and letters that have gone in vain. One in particular was from a friend of the presiding judge defending his good friend for abandoning his children and not giving his wife one dime of child support for their children.

This is the same judge that has incarcerated many other dead beat dads, but I would not expect that law to apply to a federal judge.

Please help and I would be willing to travel.

Sincerely,
John Vaglica

I did not hear from the doctor, his wife, or any of his staff either accepting or denying my pleas for help. I wrote to the doctor's show two more times to no avail. In my last-ditch effort for some desperate help, I wrote a fourth and final letter, which read as follows:

April 15, 2009

Dear Dr.

This is my fourth attempt to contact you to appear on your show since I was in litigation against my former employer back in April of 2008. Since then I have been investigating the federal judge extensively for his refusal to allow the jury to hear most of the basis of my lawsuit. I am begging for your help and do not know why I have not heard back from you. I watch your show every day and have seen you help people less desperate than myself for answers. I have totally lost all faith in our judicial system and the willingness for anyone to let the truth prevail.

You are my last resort and I hope that after reading my case you will help. Please help and I would be willing to travel.

Sincerely,

John Vaglica

Since I did not hear from the doctor or any representative of his show in this last appeal for help, I could only conclude that there was a fear on their part because of his ties to the Houston area. I have always felt that, at the very least, I should have been extended the courtesy of being contacted by some team member of the doctor's show informing me of their denial or acceptance of help or support. I have no fear of exposing any wrongdoings even if the wrongdoings are at the hand of a federal judge. I decided to abort the assistance of any outside help. I now knew I had to tell my own story, although painful at times.

Well, after the two e-mails from the ex-judge, I could only sit back in amazement. Amazement with the fact that here are two lawyers, one that had been a judge and the second is still on the bench. They are both condoning nonsupport by a federal judge for his children. Additionally, the thought for a lawsuit for contractual alimony against the judge's ex-wife had been entered into their minds.

When I originally began writing this book, it was for revenge. I began writing to tell all the people in Houston, Texas, about the injustice in our judicial system. I wanted everyone to know what happened to me because of a vengeful judge that used his power and his bigotry. Then I realized I would be as vengeful as he is, and I do not want to become that person.

Furthermore, my story is not about losing a trial, and it is not about a vengeful judge. It is about bigotry, hatred, and prejudice. It is about people growing up in an era when you could not be the person you are in your own skin. Unfortunately, this situation still exists and breeds today.

I would hate to think that the rules of this world only apply to the common folks and not judges. It would be a shame to think that all federal judges operate their lives in the manner that this judge has displayed in living his, without character or integrity. He has to live with himself, and he has to look at himself at the end of the day. I further agonized over writing this book but knew after I investigated all the facts that I had a story to tell. If I get no other satisfaction in writing this book, it will be to shed this injustice from my shoulders, and perhaps I can finally move on with my life.

I made the determination that someone needed to take accountability for this travesty of justice that was forced upon me. I took accountability to ensure that my story was told and now hope that the readers of this book will understand that the rights of the gay population are still in jeopardy by bigots.

These are my memoir's readers, with nothing held back. My life is now an open book. I have overcome the adversities and the hatred, the bigotry and the prejudice. It has taken me two years since the trial to get to this point, but I have patience and I am a survivor.

About The Author

JOHN PETER VAGLICA was raised in Newton, Massachusetts. He has a certification in human resources management from Bentley College in Waltham, Massachusetts. He also holds a master's certification in program management from George Washington University in Washington, D.C. The author and his partner, Kirk Holland, have been together seven years now. They reside in the Woodlands, Texas.

www.ingramcontent.com/pod-product-compliance
Lightning Source LLC
Chambersburg PA
CBHW020342290526
45785CB00005B/2135